*V*isiting the *P*ast

The Acropolis

Jane Shuter

Heinemann
LIBRARY

First published in Great Britain by Heinemann Library,
Halley Court, Jordan Hill, Oxford OX2 8EJ,
a division of Reed Educational and Professional Publishing Ltd.
Heinemann is a registered trademark of Reed Educational & Professional Publishing Limited.

OXFORD MELBOURNE AUCKLAND
JOHANNESBURG BLANTYRE GABORONE
IBADAN PORTSMOUTH NH (USA) CHICAGO

Designed by Visual Image
Illustrations by David Cuzick and Visual Image
Printed in Hong Kong

03 02 01 00 99
10 9 8 7 6 5 4 3 2 1

ISBN 0 431 02775 7

British Library Cataloguing in Publication Data

Shuter, Jane
    The Acropolis. – (Visiting the past)
    1. Acropolis (Athens, Greece) – Juvenile literature
    I. Title
    938.5
    ISBN 0431 02775 7

Acknowledgements

The Publishers would like to thank Richard Butcher and Magnet Harlequin for permission to reproduce all
photographs, apart from those on pages 14, 16 and 26, which are reproduced with permission of the
Acropolis Museum.

Cover photograph reproduced with permission of AKG London.

The Publishers would like to thank Joe Scott for his comments in the preparation of this title.

Every effort has been made to contact copyright holders of any material reproduced in this book. Any
omissions will be rectified in subsequent printings if notice is given to the Publisher.

For more information about Heinemann Library books, or to order, please phone ++44(0)1865 888066, or
send a fax to ++44(0)1865 314091. You can visit our website at www.heinemann.co.uk.

Any words appearing in the text in bold, **like this**, are explained in the Glossary.

Contents

A place of safety

Most Greek cities were built around an **acropolis**, a hilltop fortress or **citadel**. The most famous of these is in Athens. It covers just over four hectares, with a flattish area on the top measuring 268 metres by 93 metres. The Acropolis is famous for the **temples** and buildings that remain on it today; but it has been lived on and used over thousands of years. The buildings have been constantly repaired and replaced. They tell us a lot about how ancient Greek builders worked and give us an insight into ancient Greek ideas and beliefs.

The first people to use the Acropolis, from about 3000BC, used it as a safe place to live because it was high up and hard to get to. Its flattish top was easier to build on, and it had fresh-water springs – which meant that people did not have to keep hauling water up from the plains below. In about 1250BC a king moved on to the Acropolis, making it a target for his enemies. The natural defence of the steep, rocky climb no longer provided enough protection. The king had strong, stone walls built to **fortify** the sides of the Acropolis.

From the top of the Acropolis, people could see the countryside all around. The modern city of Athens covers most of that countryside now.

4

A place of worship

Hundreds of years passed. Athens grew and people moved down from the Acropolis to farm the plains around it. Greece developed into several **city states**, including Athens, which often fought each other. The Athenians still used the Acropolis in times of danger, but its main use was as a place for worshipping the gods. The first temples were wooden but, in about 675BC, the first stone temples were built, including one to the goddess after whom the city was named – Athena. In these buildings, and in the spaces between them, there were statues and places to make **offerings** to the various gods and goddesses.

Athens in peril

In 490BC the Persians, who were old enemies of the Greek city states, attacked, but were beaten by the heavily outnumbered Athenians at Marathon. The Athenians started a huge, new temple on the Acropolis, to thank Athena for their victory. The Persians, meanwhile, plotted revenge. The new temple had barely risen above its stone **foundations** when, ten years later, the Persians were back – determined to conquer all of Greece. They burned Athens to the ground and destroyed everything on the Acropolis, but the Greeks finally drove them off in a sea battle at Salamis.

The Athenians rebuilt their ruined city and repaired the Acropolis walls. Those Athenians who had fought the Persians decided not to repair their destroyed temples, but to leave them as a reminder of what had happened.

The ruins of the oldest stone temple to Athena are in the lower half of this photograph.

Classical times

Many **city states** felt that the Persians were still dangerous after the battle of Salamis, so they made an **alliance** called the Delian League. The Athenians, who had the biggest **fleet**, were asked to lead it. Each city state had to send ships to Athens to form part of a navy – most gave money instead. Athens became more and more rich and powerful, and dominated the city states of the League.

In about 449BC Athens made peace with Persia. The Athenian leader, Pericles, wanted to rebuild the **temples** on the **Acropolis** – partly to please the gods, partly to show how rich and powerful Athens was. He called a meeting of all other city states that had fought the Persians, to discuss keeping the seas safe and whether to rebuild the temples. No one came. They resented Athens' growing power and did not want Pericles to order them about. Pericles had expected this and announced that the Athenians would decide for everyone – the Delian League had to go on paying Athens money for the navy, and the temples could be rebuilt.

Building the Parthenon

In 448BC the Athenian Assembly met and approved the plans for the Parthenon – a new temple to replace the one begun over 40 years before, after the Athenian victory at Marathon. By now there was even more to thank Athena for: the victory at Marathon, later victories over the Persians and growing power over the other city states. The Parthenon, and the statue of Athena inside it, would have to be very grand indeed to show enough gratitude.

Building work began in 448BC. Despite interruptions, it was finished by 432BC. It was as beautiful and awe-inspiring as Pericles had hoped, a wonderful **offering** to the goddess and an impressive display of the wealth and power of Athens.

The Great Panathenaia was celebrated every four years in Athens. A huge procession took a new robe to the statue of Athena on the Acropolis.

Destruction and reconstruction

For almost a thousand years the **Acropolis** remained almost untouched. When the Romans added Athens to their empire in 86BC they did not destroy it, as the Persians had done, for they admired it, especially the Parthenon. Tourists came to Athens from all over the **Roman Empire** – they even bought copies of the huge statue of Athena in the Parthenon as souvenirs! The Romans kept the Greek **temples** repaired and added a few statues and a small circular **shrine** to Roman gods.

Athens remained part of the Roman Empire for many hundreds of years. As the power of Rome declined, it had a number of different rulers before the Turks took over in about 1455. During this time the temples of the Acropolis were used for Christian and, later, Muslim worship.

Turkish gunpowder

Because the Acropolis was the safest place for miles around, the Turks stacked the Propylaea (the buildings at the entrance) and the Parthenon with weapons and **gunpowder**. Unfortunately, nature and the Venetians (old enemies of the Turks) both brought disaster. In 1656 lightning struck the gunpowder store in the Propylaea, blowing it apart. In 1687 a bombardment by the Venetians ignited more gunpowder and the Parthenon, too, was blown apart. The Venetians took over Athens, temporarily.

The biggest alteration to the Acropolis in Roman times was a monument to the Roman general Agrippa, made by the Greeks to thank him for helping Athens when it was threatened by barbarians. This is the reconstructed base of that monument.

The Acropolis is constantly being repaired and restored. This is partly to repair damage done by the weather and bad pollution levels of Athens, and also to make the buildings more as they were before the explosions.

Until 1687, most of the buildings on the Acropolis had been well preserved. Now, people thought the Acropolis' treasures were up for grabs. The Turks recaptured Athens, but did not try to repair any of the damage. Many of the statues and carvings, even the smashed chunks of **marble**, were taken away – as stone for building, to crush and burn to make lime (for building and other uses) and as souvenirs. Before 1687 there had been 20 human statues and two horses on the western side of the Parthenon. By 1800 there were only four human statues left.

In 1801 the Turks gave the British **ambassador**, Lord Elgin, permission to take whatever he wanted from the Acropolis. Elgin, who was horrified by the way that the Acropolis was being **ransacked**, decided that the treasures of the Acropolis would be better off in British care. He shipped many carvings from the Parthenon back to England, where they can still be seen in the British Museum in London.

In 1833 the Greeks eventually drove the Turks out of Athens. They began to **restore** the Acropolis. They pulled down all the buildings that had been added by the Turks and other invaders, and began to rebuild and restore the temples as accurately as they could. This work still continues today.

Workers try to use ancient Greek building techniques, but they use modern technology too – such as the metal scaffolding and crane in the picture. Visitors used to be able to walk around the temples of the Acropolis. Now they are roped off, to stop people climbing all over them.

*I*deas about the gods

The ancient Greeks worshipped many different gods and goddesses. They saw these gods and goddesses as very like ordinary people; more beautiful, far more powerful, but driven by the same emotions. There is no holy book, like the *Bible* or the *Koran*, that tells us about their religion. But the ancient Greeks did have myths (stories about the gods) which have been passed down so we can read or listen to them today. The **Acropolis** gives us clues about ancient Greek religion too.

Athena vs Poseidon

Many ancient Greek cities had a god or goddess to take special care of their city. However, they did not ignore the other gods, that would make them angry. According to myth, Athena, the goddess of war and wisdom, and Poseidon, the god of the sea, fought over who would be the special protector of Athens. The myth says Athena and Poseidon fought on the Acropolis. Poseidon stuck his trident into the ground and a salt-water spring erupted. Athena stuck her spear into the ground and an olive tree sprung up. Athena won. Some versions of the myth say that the chief god, Zeus, decided she had won, others say the Athenians voted on it.

The first statue of Athena worshipped on the Acropolis was said to be carved from the wood of the olive tree she made spring from the ground. The Greeks did not think the statue was the goddess, but they did think that they had to treat it with as much care as if it was – to show Athena how much they cared for her.

This olive tree stands where the first olive tree, said to have sprung from Athena's spear, stood. Some people say it is a shoot from the same roots.

10

The Acropolis and the city

The Acropolis tells us that the gods and goddesses the ancient Greeks worshipped were very important. The Athenians used the most visible, highest, best-defended place for their **temples**. They built their homes and public buildings around the Acropolis. The gods could look out over the city, and the **citizens** could look up from their daily life and be reminded of the gods.

There were temples, **shrines** and other places to worship in Athens itself, as well as on the Acropolis; but the Acropolis was the most important religious site. It was where all the big, public, religious festivals took place and where the sacred statue of Athena was kept.

The ancient Greeks built their temples to last. They were carefully made from expensive, heavy **marble**. Even the later explosions that ruined parts of the Acropolis did not destroy the buildings completely. The public buildings in Athens were made from marble too, because they were important to the Athenians. The Athenians' own homes were made of sun-baked, mud bricks on stone **foundations**, with walls that were soft and crumbled so easily that burglars were called 'wall piercers'. The Greeks' homes were much less permanent than their temples.

Even in modern Athens, with its tall buildings, the Acropolis still dominates the skyline.

The oldest buildings in Athens are in the area around the Acropolis. But even these only date back a few hundred years. None of the ordinary homes of ancient Athens have survived.

How did temples work?

Ancient Greek **temples** were not like the churches, synagogues or mosques of other religions. They were not places that people went into to worship. They were, instead, places where statues and other **artefacts** of the gods or goddesses of the temple were put, cared for by priests or priestesses. They were, in a way, homes for the gods. The ancient Greeks did not believe that the gods really lived in these temples, but they believed that acting as if they did showed the gods respect. Temples were designed to be beautiful. The gods were believed to enjoy looking at beautiful things, like buildings and statues.

The ancient Greeks did worship at temples, but they worshipped outside. Religious ceremonies always included prayers and **sacrifices** at altars, often to the east of the temple. Temples were designed so that the statue of the god could look out of the end of the temple towards the altar, to 'see' the sacrifice.

The gods could look out of the doorways of temples, from the inner room, to the sacrifices taking place outside.

If people could not go into the temples, how did they worship their gods? There were many different ways to worship. People could say a quiet prayer by a statue or **shrine** to a particular god or goddess. They could leave something they valued there as an **offering**, which varied depending on how rich the giver was and what they wanted from the gods. Offerings did not have to be expensive to please the gods, but they had to mean a lot to the giver – such as a string of cheap beads given to them by someone they loved.

Religious festivals

The big religious festivals were held on the **Acropolis**. People marched up to the Acropolis along the Panathenic Way, the main path to the Acropolis from the city, to pray outside the temple and watch the sacrifices. They ate the meat of the animals that were sacrificed as part of the ceremony.

Big festivals lasted several days, and were not just sacrifices and prayers. There were musical performances. There were plays performed at the theatres. There were sporting competitions: races, wrestling and throwing competitions. These things were not done just for fun but as offerings to the gods.

The most direct way to the Acropolis from the **agora**, the main square of the city. There were other routes to the Acropolis, including the Panathenic Way, used during the yearly festival for Athena.

The theatre of Dionysus (god of wine) just below the walls of the Acropolis, where plays were performed for religious festivals.

13

Ideas about war

Greek **city states** were small and did not have full-time armies. They expected all men to fight when the city state was threatened either by other city states or by foreign enemies, like the Persians. Most Greek men would fight for their city state at least once in their lives. Ancient Greek stories were full of battles and heroic deeds. Men were expected to fight bravely and if they died defending their city state, then they were honoured.

The **Acropolis** tells us about the ancient Greeks and war in several ways. The fact that the city state grew up around the Acropolis, a defensive site, tells us that the Greeks were always poised for war, trying to guard against attack. Also, the goddess they chose as the special protector of the city, and worshipped on the Acropolis, was a warrior goddess. Athena was worshipped in several different ways in ancient Greece: she was the goddess of wisdom, but she was also the goddess of war and of victory, as Athena Nike, and was shown with a helmet, spear and shield to emphasize this fact.

The Athenians thought that Athena's warlike nature would be good for the city she guarded and would bring them victory.

Honouring the brave

The Acropolis also tells us that the Athenians believed in honouring the men who died fighting for it. Athena did not always bring victory, sometimes even the buildings on the Acropolis were destroyed. But, to the Athenians, victories and defeats had to be remembered, and those who fought and died had to be honoured.

So when the Persians took Athens in 480BC, stone from the destroyed **temples** on the Acropolis was used to repair its walls. Stones from the **columns** of the temple to Athena were set into the repaired walls where they could be seen from the **agora**, or main square. They were both an early war memorial and a warning to the people of the city to be on their guard.

The Athenians celebrated victories too. The decorative carvings on the Parthenon show one of the festivals to Athena held every four years, the Great Panathenaia. Historians think that it shows the last Panathenaia before the great battle of Marathon against the Persians in 490BC. It celebrates the victory at Marathon, that the Greeks believed Athena helped them win, and also remembers the men who died there.

The reused columns from behind, inside the Acropolis. If you look closely you can just see the decorated edge on the column marked.

The Acropolis from the agora. The reused columns are on the left.

15

Reflecting real life?

The **Acropolis** tells us about Greek ideas about the gods and war. It also tells us, as we shall see, a lot about ancient Greek building methods. Does it tell us anything about the people themselves, their everyday life? In some ways, it cannot do this. For much of its existence it was not a place where people lived, or even visited daily. But there are some things we can find out.

The carvings, especially those on the Parthenon, show what people looked like – how they dressed and styled their hair. They also show some furniture, jars and boxes. Most of these carvings are no longer on the Parthenon, nor even in the museum on the Acropolis. Those that have not been destroyed have been scattered across the world. A large collection of carvings, the Elgin Marbles, is in the British Museum. However, the Acropolis Museum has **artefacts** from several time periods, which give interesting information.

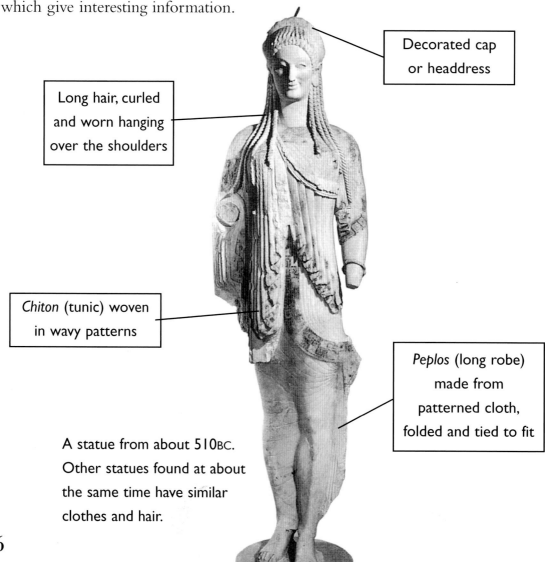

Decorated cap or headdress

Long hair, curled and worn hanging over the shoulders

Chiton (tunic) woven in wavy patterns

Peplos (long robe) made from patterned cloth, folded and tied to fit

A statue from about 510BC. Other statues found at about the same time have similar clothes and hair.

Athenian clothing

In some ways the women shown are dressed very similarly, considering that the statues were made a century apart. They look much more alike than a woman from 1899 and one from 1999 would do. They have long, loose clothing, which has lots of drapes and folds. Their hair is long and worn in a complicated style. There are changes in the way the clothes are fastened and the way the hair is fixed, but the general style was the one that was best for the climate, so no one saw the need to change the design much.

Men wore similar clothes, indeed, in poorer families, men and women of similar size often shared clothing. The differences in clothes were more to do with wealth than sex. Poorer men and women, who needed to work in their clothes, wore shorter, simpler tunics. The rich wore the longer, more draped styles.

Long hair, styled in ringlets

Long robe, loosely draped, tied at the waist and fastened at the shoulders. Not tied up in the same way as the earlier *peplos*.

The cloth could have been patterned. The decoration is long gone from the original statues.

One of the female statues supporting a porch of the Erechtheion **temple** of the Acropolis. It is an exact copy: the originals were either stolen or badly damaged by air pollution. The originals were made in about 409BC. Other statues found at about the same time have similar clothes and hair.

Beautiful buildings

The ancient Greeks had a very mathematical view of beautiful architecture. They thought that the most beautiful buildings were **symmetrical** and in proportion. Every measurement had to balance and work in relation to every other measurement. Only then would the building look right. This applied to all buildings – theatres and public buildings as well as **temples**.

A perfect example of this is the Parthenon, the biggest and most important temple on the **Acropolis**. Pericles wanted it to be the most beautiful and perfect temple ever built. The proportions of the Parthenon, shown in the picture below, were worked out very carefully so that everything worked out at a **ratio** of nine to four. The measurements marked on the photo show what this means. The length and width of the temple fitted this ratio too, although we cannot see them on this photo.

This photo of the Parthenon shows how the ancient Greeks' use of ratios worked in practice. The height of the columns (A) is four-ninths the width of the Parthenon (B). The width of each column (C) is four-ninths the distance between them (D).

Building in style

Proportion was important, but this does not mean that everything on an ancient Greek building measured exactly straight. They had to *look* elegant and in proportion, and sometimes this meant using little tricks in the building.

The floor of the Parthenon rises very slightly in the centre and the **columns** get narrower towards the top – seemingly in a smooth line. To create this effect, the builders had to make a bulge in the columns about two-thirds of the way up. Also the columns do not go straight up, they tilt inwards slightly. All these changes mean that the building does not look like a square-sided box. It looks elegant and in proportion.

The square sides of the photograph help you to see how the column angles tilt. The changes in floor level and column width are probably too small to notice in a photo.

Architects thought that temples needed to be raised up, so they could be seen, but not so high that they could not be looked at comfortably. Almost all temples have three marble steps up, on top of low foundations of ordinary stone.

Builders at work

Ancient Greek builders paid just as much attention to detail as architects did. They thought it was important that the visitor's gaze flowed smoothly over a beautiful building. They made sure that each brick, or piece of a **column**, fitted together so that the finished wall, or column, looked as though it was made from a single piece of **marble**. They wanted the joins to be as invisible as possible. Despite only having a few simple, iron tools and very basic lifting equipment, they still managed to do this.

Builders took great care over the visible parts of their buildings. Parts that were not going to be seen, however, did not have to be beautiful. They just had to work. So when it was decided that the Parthenon would be bigger than originally planned, the builders extended the **foundations** using whatever stone came to hand to make a flat surface – they did not bother to match up the size of the stone with the old foundations. The foundations were not meant to be seen.

The ground level on the Acropolis is lower now than it would have been in ancient times, mainly due to damage and **erosion**. It is now possible to see the foundations of the Parthenon and how they were extended.

The fixings that held the marble or stone blocks together were on the inside, and could not be seen on the finished building. Because several buildings on the **Acropolis** were damaged, we can see how the builders worked by examining pieces of marble that are no longer part of the building.

This iron clamp, used in a modern piece of restoration, was not covered in lead. It has started to rust.

This block was joined to the next one by an iron clamp that fitted into this T-shaped hole. The ancient Greek builders covered each clamp in lead, which kept the water out and stopped the iron from rusting.

This piece of marble was deliberately roughened, so that the piece that went over it gripped tightly.

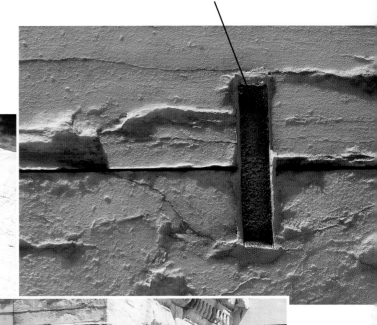

The wall to the right is damaged, so the joins are more evident, but even after thousands of years the blocks still fit together tightly.

Columns

The ancient Greeks used two sorts of **column** to hold up their buildings, Doric columns and Ionic columns. There are examples of both on the **Acropolis**, used to deliberately contrast with each other. So the Parthenon, designed to be a substantial, imposing building, has Doric columns. The Erechtheion nearby has Ionic columns; it was smaller and made a deliberate contrast with the Parthenon. The Propylaea entrance used both sorts of column.

Ionic columns (shown below), which were more ornate, with a decorated base and **capital**, and slimmer than Doric columns. This style was particularly associated with Athens and eastern Greece.

Doric columns (shown above), which sit directly on the floor of the **temple** and have a plain capital at the top.

This column has been rebuilt as carefully as possible, but the damage done over time means that you can see that it is made up of several different drums. The picture below shows the way the columns would have joined together tightly and evenly.

The column drum was cut into shape at the **quarry**. The handles sticking out of the side are for the ropes slung around it to lift it into place. These lifting handles were chipped off once the column was in place. Each piece was fixed to the one below it by a fixing pin in a hole in the centre.

This is a drum from the bottom of a column. The part facing us would have sat directly on the floor of the temple. We know this, because it has no fixing hole to secure it to the next drum down. Also, the edges have been **fluted** (shaped). Fluting was done once all the drums were in place, except for the bottom drum, where enough was fluted at the very bottom to mean that the fluting ran all the way to the floor.

Finishing off

Once all the parts of the **temple** were in place, it was time for the finishing off. Before the decorative carvings and the statues were put in place, craftsmen had to **flute** the **columns**, decorate the tops and bottoms of the columns and tile the roof. They also had to do any carving around doorways or on ceilings.

Fluting was hugely time consuming and took a great deal of skill. It did not make the columns any stronger, but it did make them more beautiful. And, of course, the gods would know how hard it was to do and how long it took, and would appreciate the skill that went into it.

Doric and Ionic columns had different kinds of fluting, both done after the column drums had been fitted together, so that each flute made one smooth sweep down the column. Doric columns have 20 flutes, which meet each other at a sharp edge. Ionic columns, though narrower, have more flutes – 24 of them, separated from each other by a smooth band.

The carved ceiling of the Erechtheion. You can also see the decorative carving on the wall and over the door.

The base of this Ionic column of the Erechtheion has been decorated. You can also see the flutes and the flattened band that separates them.

Roofing the Parthenon

The roofs of almost all ancient Greek houses, public buildings and temples were made from **terracotta**, shaped in moulds and left to dry in the sun. The roof of the Parthenon, however, was covered with **marble** tiles, so that even the roof shone in the sun. Although marble tiles were made to the same design and fixed to the roof in the same way as terracotta tiles, they gave the builders special problems.

Marble was far heavier than terracotta, and much more difficult to make roof tiles from. The tiles could not be too thick – or they would be so heavy that the roof would not be able to take the weight. They could not be made too thin or wide either, or they would crack too easily. They might even split while they were being made. So they had to be made fairly small.

The wider tiles were put on the wooden roof frame, with their curved edges facing upwards.

Smaller V-shaped tiles were then put on top, to hold the edges of the bottom tiles together.

The **restorers** have found some marble roof tiles and put them together to show visitors to the Acropolis how they worked. Many of the older buildings in Athens are roofed in terracotta tiles using the same system.

These decorated end-pieces (antefixes) stood along the end of the roof, to help hold the tiles in place.

Statues and carvings

The buildings and scattered pieces of **marble** on the **Acropolis** can give us a good idea about the building process. They tell us less about what the finished buildings would have looked like when they were filled with statues and covered with carvings, all beautifully painted and decorated with gold. While the skill of Greek builders and **sculptors** is admired, we know very little about the skill of their painters; indeed, many people do not even realize that many statues and buildings were once painted.

There are two main reasons for this. Firstly, over the thousands of years, time, environmental pollution and general wear and tear have worn away much of the colour from the marble that is left. Secondly, there are only a few original statues and carvings on the site. These are in the museum, where they are kept safe from further attacks by the weather and pollution. Many of the statues and carvings have been taken away to museums and other places all over the world, and even these have largely lost their colour. So when you next look at a Greek statue, or a picture of one, try to imagine what it would have looked like when it was beautifully painted.

From earliest times the carvings on the Acropolis were painted to make them more colourful. These figures come from the eastern side of the Parthenon.

We do know that a huge number of sculptors worked on the site, carving all the decorative carvings. Some of them were better than others. All of them could, of course, carve figures that looked like people and horses, but some of these figures were incredibly life-like.

Unlike most sculptures that decorate buildings, the ones on the Parthenon were carved as if they were statues, not flat at the back. The details on the backs of the carvings are just as carefully sculpted as the fronts, despite the fact that, in most cases, they would never be seen. This is another example of the desire to make this building absolutely perfect, reflecting both the glory of the city state of Athens and its people's gratitude to their protector Athena.

There is still some carving left on the Parthenon. This is part of a series, showing a **mythological** battle between centaurs (half-man, half-horse) and humans. It was made by one of the best sculptors, and looks very life-like and full of movement.

The other carving still in place on the Parthenon, on the pediment over the front porch. It is part of the myth of the birth of Athena.

27

Timeline

c.3000BC	First settlement established on the **Acropolis**
1250BC	Palace built on the Acropolis, for Mycenaean king. Walls are built to strengthen the natural defences of the hill.
675BC	First stone **temples** built on the Acropolis
490BC	Persian invasion of Greece defeated at the battle of Marathon
480BC	Persian invasion of Greece defeated at the battle of Salamis
449BC	Athenians make peace with Persia
448BC	Plans approved for building the Parthenon
447BC	Parthenon begun
432BC	Parthenon finished
86BC	Athens becomes part of the **Roman Empire**
AD269	Romans driven out of Athens. The invading barbarians, Goths, take over for a while. Various tribes then control the city. These include Christians, who use the Acropolis as a fort and build a Christian church inside the Parthenon.
1455	Turks take over Athens
1656	Propylaea damaged by **gunpowder** explosion, set off by lightning
1687	Parthenon damaged by explosion caused by gunpowder set off by Venetian attack
1801	Turks allow Lord Elgin to remove the sculptures on the Parthenon, which are now in the British Museum and known as the Elgin Marbles
1833	Athens comes under Greek control

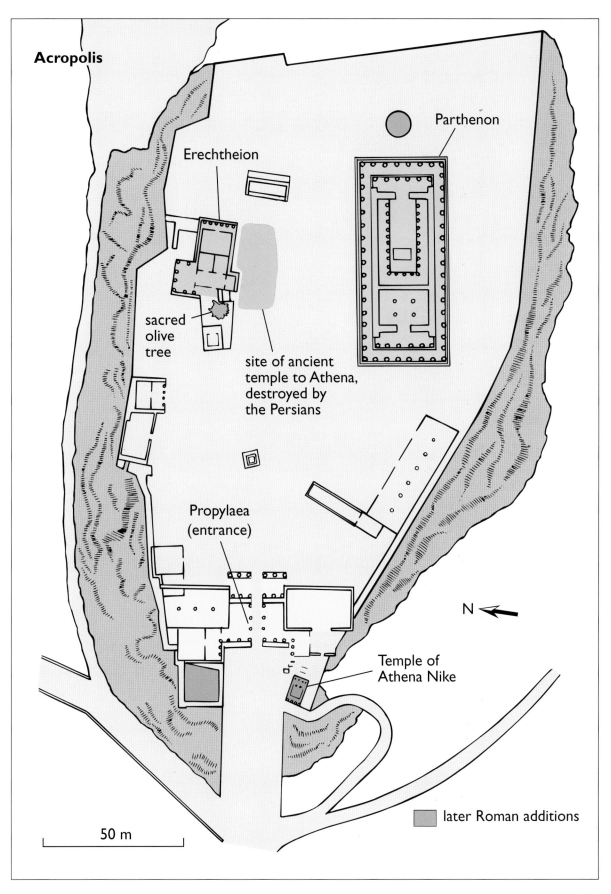

Acropolis

Parthenon

Erechtheion

sacred olive tree

site of ancient temple to Athena, destroyed by the Persians

Propylaea (entrance)

N ←

Temple of Athena Nike

50 m

later Roman additions

Glossary

acropolis hilltop fortress in ancient Greece. The Acropolis at Athens is the most famous.

agora main square of a city in ancient Greece

alliance agreement between different people or groups of people to work together for a common goal

ambassador person who goes to another country to act as a representative for his or her own country

artefact something made by humans, often of a historical or religious significance

capital head of a pillar or column

citadel the fortified centre of a town or city

citizen person who is part of a city state or country, protected by its laws and taking part in running it

city state independent state made up of a city and the countryside around it

column cylinder-shaped support for the roof of a building

erosion process of being worn away over time, often by the weather

fleet group of ships under the control of one commander

fluting decorative grooves that run from top to bottom on a column

foundations stone base for a building

gunpowder mixture of saltpetre, charcoal and sulphur that explodes when lit. It is used for firing bullets and cannon balls.

marble very hard kind of limestone, which can be polished to become shiny and smooth

mythological according to a traditional myth or story

offering something given to the gods as a show of respect or gratitude

quarry place where stone is dug out of the ground, usually to be used for building work

ransack to search thoroughly or violently, especially when robbing a building

ratio way of multiplying groups of numbers so that they all fit the same pattern. The following number pairs all fit a ratio of 3:1 – 3:1; 6:2; 9:3; 12:4.

restore to put something that has been changed back into its original form

Roman Empire area conquered by the Roman armies, beginning in about 510BC, which circled the Mediterranean Sea and stretched from Britain in the north to Egypt in the south. The Roman Empire began to weaken in about AD200.

sacrifice living offering. Sacrifices were killed on altars near temples to please the gods.

sculptor person who carves stone into statues or decorations on buildings

shrine special place dedicated to a god or goddess, not as grand as a temple

symmetry exact match between the opposite halves of a figure or building

temple religious building built to honour a god or goddess

terracotta mud shaped while wet and then baked hard. Terracotta is usually a reddish colour.

Index